A CHILD'S OWN BOOK OF VERSE, BOOK TWO

A CHILD'S OWN BOOK OF VERSE

BOOK TWO

BY
ADA M· SKINNER
ST. AGATHA'S SCHOOL
AND
FRANCES GILLESPY WICKES
ST. AGATHA'S SCHOOL

Illustrated by MAUD S· FULLER
and MICHAEL PETERSHAM

YESTERDAY'S CLASSICS
CHAPEL HILL, NORTH CAROLINA

This edition, first published in 2006 by Yesterday's Classics, is an unabridged republication of the work originally published by The Macmillan Company in 1917. For a complete listing of books published by Yesterday's Classics, visit www.yesterdaysclassics.com. Yesterday's Classics is the publishing arm of the Baldwin Project which presents the complete text of dozens of classic books for children at www.mainlesson.com under the editorship of Lisa M. Ripperton and T. A. Roth.

ISBN-10: 1-59915-052-2

ISBN-13: 978-1-59915-052-9

Yesterday's Classics
PO Box 3418
Chapel Hill, NC 27515

ACKNOWLEDGMENTS

THANKS are due to Chas. Scribner's Sons for permission to use "The Night Wind" by Eugene Field; to L. C. Page Co. for permission to use "Prince Tatters" by Laura E. Richards; to the Youth's Companion for permission to use "The Quest" by Eudora Bumstead; to Mrs. Richard Watson Gilder for "Christmas Tree in the Nursery" by Richard Watson Gilder; to Charles E. Carryl for "The Plaint of the Camel"; to Ann B. Warner for "Ready for Duty"; to Bliss Carman for "Mr. Moon"; to E. V. Lucas for permission to use "Snow in Town"; to Fred E. Weatherley for permission to use "The Gray Doves' Answer"; to The Macmillan Co. for permission to use "The Twilight" by Madison Cawein and the "Four-Leaf Clover" by Ella Higginson. The selections from Lucy Larcom, Abbie Farwell Brown, Margaret Deland, Celia Thaxter, and Frank Dempster Sherman are used by permission of, and by special arrangement with, Houghton Mifflin Co., the authorized publishers of their works.

TABLE OF CONTENTS

INTRODUCTION

"I know not how it is that we need an interpreter, but the great majority of men seem to be . . . mutes, who cannot report the conversation they have had with nature." "The poet is the sayer, the namer, and represents beauty." "The poets are liberating gods. . . . They are free and make free."

(Poetry—Emerson.)

THEN let us use the poets, wisely, freely, fully to liberate the souls of our children, to make them free.

Never were we in graver peril of forgetting our poets, of losing their liberating influence, of dulling, benumbing our sense of beauty than at present; for modern education, pressed by economic needs, confronted with industrial exigencies, dominated by the scientific spirit of the age which exults in marvels of mechanical invention, is rapidly tending to extol efficiency as its exclusive pursuit, forgetting the eternal need of beauty in human life, if man is to be more than a human mechanism, unmindful that starvation of the soul is more fatal than starvation of the body.

Poetry rather than prose is the language of childhood, Mother Goose is the child's first "liberating god." But with Mother Goose the process of liberation is only begun. Systematically should it be continued, throughout the whole period of education.

To facilitate the systematic use of poetry in the classroom, *A Child's Own Book of Verse* has been compiled. Attention is called to the fact that it is the child's own book, not the teacher's, because the child's interests have been a guiding principle of selection. Variations in taste and in temperament have prompted the inclusion of a wide variety of poems, not always classic in quality, that every "open sesame" to the great world of poetry might be offered.

The earliest appeal is to the ear through sound rhymes, jingles, rhythm. In the next stage sound rhymes and rhythm are connected with personal experience as in imitative poems, such as "The Wind." Next have been added poems in which thought plays an equal part with sound and rhythms as in lullabies and pure lyrics. These are followed by story-telling poems.

A Child's Own Book of Verse consists of three volumes planned for use during the four primary years.

BOOK ONE is made up of sound rhymes, lyrics, and story-telling poems.

BOOK TWO follows much the same plan. Less space is given to sound rhymes and more to lyrics and longer story-telling poems with the addition of a group of short descriptive poems.

BOOK THREE has many of the features of the first and second books, but it contains, in addition, a larger group of descriptive poems, and many of the longer simple ballads are included.

It is hoped that by so constant and so thoughtful a use of verse as these volumes suggest there may result a liberating of the sense of beauty, an instilling of an abiding love of poetry, the interpreter of beauty, and, it may be, a freeing of the power of poetic expression.

EMMA J. SEBRING.

ST. AGATHA

A SEA SONG FROM THE SHORE

Hail! Ho!
Sail! Ho!
Ahoy! Ahoy! Ahoy!
Who calls to me,
So far at sea?
Only a little boy!

Sail! Ho!
Hail! Ho!
The sailor he sails the sea:

1

I wish he would capture
A little sea-horse
And send him home to me.

I wish, as he sails
Through the tropical gales,
He would catch me a sea-bird, too,
With its silver wings
And the song it sings,
And its breast of down and dew!

I wish he would catch me a
Little mermaid,
Some island where he lands,
With her dripping curls,
And her crown of pearls,
And the looking-glass in her hands!

Hail! Ho!
Sail! Ho!
Sail far o'er the fabulous main!
And if I were a sailor,
I 'd sail with you,
Though I never sailed back again.
—JAMES WHITCOMB RILEY.

THE NIGHT WIND

Have you ever heard the wind go "Yooooo"?
   'T is a pitiful sound to hear!
It seems to chill you through and through
   With a strange and speechless fear.
'T is the voice of the night that broods outside
   When folks should be asleep,
And many and many 's the time I 've cried
To the darkness brooding far and wide
   Over the land and the deep:
"Whom do you want, O lonely night,
That you wail the long hours through?"
And the night would say in its ghostly way:

   "Yoooooooo!
   Yoooooooo!
   Yoooooooo!"

My mother told me long ago
   (When I was a little tad)
That when the night went wailing so,
   Somebody had been bad;
And then, when I was snug in bed,
   Whither I had been sent,
With blankets pulled up 'round my head,
I 'd think of what my mother 'd said,
   And wonder what boy she meant!
And "Who's been bad to-day?" I 'd ask

3

Of the wind that hoarsely blew,
And the voice would say in its meaningful way:

"Yooooooooo!
Yooooooooo!
Yooooooooo!"

That this was true I must allow—
    You 'll not believe it, though!
Yes, though I 'm quite a model now,
    I was not always so.
And if you doubt what things I say,
    Suppose you make the test;
Suppose, when you 've been bad some day
And up to bed are sent away
    From mother and the rest—
Suppose you ask, "Who has been bad?"
    And then you 'll hear what 's true;
For the wind will moan in its ruefulest tone:

"Yooooooooo!
Yooooooooo!
Yooooooooo!"

—Eugene Field.

BUMBLE-BEE AND CLOVER

Came a roaring bumble-bee,
Pockets full of money.
"Ah, good morning, Clover sweet,
What 's the price of honey?"

4

"Help yourself, sir," Clover said,
"Bumble, you 're too funny;
Never Clover yet so poor
She must sell her honey."

TWINKLING BUGS

When the sun sinks under the world's red rim,
And the river fades till its shores are dim,
And the trees are dark where the shadows lie,
    Then they go by,
        By,
            By—
The twinkling bugs go by.

They trim their lamps through the daylight hours,
For each bug rubs and rubs and scours,
To have his bright as the stars in the sky,
    When they go by,
        By,
            By—
The twinkling bugs go by.

They hide so well through the whole long day,
You never can find one, search as you may;
You never need look till fades the sky,
    Then they go by,
        By,
            By—
Then twinkling bugs go by.

THE SEA SHELL

Sea Shell, Sea Shell,
Sing me a song, O please!
A song of ships and sailor-men
    Of parrots and tropical trees;
Of islands lost in the Spanish Main
Which no man may see again,
Of fishes and corals under the waves,
And sea-horses stabled in great green caves—
    Sea Shell, Sea Shell,
    Sing me a song, O please.
                                —AMY LOWELL.

THE TWILIGHT

In her wimple of wind and her slippers of sleep,
The Twilight comes like a little goose-girl,
Herding her owls with many "Tu-whoos,"
Her little brown owls in the woodland deep,
Where dimly she walks in her whispering shoes,
And gown of shimmering pearl.
                                —MADISON CAWEIN.

THE SING-AWAY BIRD

Have you ever heard of the Sing-away bird,
    That sings where the Runaway River
Runs down with its rills to the bald-headed hills
    That stand in the sunshine and shiver?
    "Oh, sing! sing-away! sing-away!"

6

How the pines and the birches are stirred
By the trill of the Sing-away bird!

'T was a white-throated sparrow, that sped a light arrow
    Of song from his musical quiver,
And it pierced with its spell every valley and dell
    On the banks of the Runaway River.
        "Oh, sing! sing-away! sing-away!"
    The song of the wild singer had
    The sound of a soul that is glad.

And the bald-headed hills, with their rocks and their rills,
    To the tune of rapture are ringing;
And their faces grow young, all the gray mists among,
    While the forests break forth into singing!
        "Oh, sing! sing-away! sing-away!"
    And the river runs singing along;
    And the flying winds catch up the song.

And, beneath the glad sun, every glad-hearted one
    Sets the world to the tune of his gladness:
The swift rivers sing it, the wild breezes wing it,
    Till Earth loses thought of her sadness.
        "Oh, sing! sing-away! sing-away!"
    Oh, sing, happy soul, to joy's Giver,
    Sing on, by Time's Runaway River!
                  —LUCY LARCOM.

WHEN THE COWS COME HOME

With klingle, klangle, klingle,
Way down the dusty dingle
The cows are coming home;

How sweet and clear, and faint and low,
The airy tinklings come and go,
Like chimings from some far-off tower,
Or patterings of an April shower
That makes the daisies grow—

Ko-kling ko-klang, koklingle lingle,
Way down the darkening dingle
The cows come slowly home.
With a klingle, klangle, klingle,
With a loo-oo and moo-oo and jingle
The cows are coming home:

And over there on Merlin's hill
Hear the plaintive cry of the whip-poor-will,
The dewdrops lie on the tangled vines,
And over the poplar Venus shines
And over the silent mill.

Ko-ling, ko-lang, kolingle lingle
With a ting-a-ling and jingle
The cows come slowly home.

Let down the bars, let in the strain
Of long-gone songs, and flowers and rain;
For dear old times come back again
When the cows come home.
—AGNES MITCHELL.

8

A LITTLE DUTCH GARDEN

I passed by a garden, a little Dutch garden,
Where useful and pretty things grew,—
Heartsease and tomatoes, and pinks and potatoes,
And lilies and onions and rue.

I saw in that garden, that little Dutch garden,
A chubby Dutch man with a spade,
And a rosy Dutch frau with a shoe like a scow,
And a flaxen-haired little Dutch maid.

There grew in that garden, that little Dutch garden,
Blue flag flowers lovely and tall,
And early blush roses, and little pink posies,
And Gretchen was fairer than all.

My heart 's in that garden, that little Dutch garden,—
It tumbled right in as I passed,
'Mid wildering mazes of spinach and daisies,
And Gretchen is holding it fast.

—HARRIET WHITNEY DURBIN.

9

MY LADY WIND

My Lady Wind is very tall,
As tall as she can be;
Her hands can shake the tallest bough
Upon the tallest tree,
And even reach up to the sky,
And twirl the clouds about,
And rattle them for thundering,
And shake the raindrops out.
And yet so light, so light she steps
Upon the flowers and grass,
They only need to bow their heads
To let my lady pass.

You cannot see my Lady Wind,
Though you can hear her plain,
And watch her tread the clovers down
That rise so quick again.
And I know just how she would look,
So tall and full of grace,
With bright hair streaming out behind,
And such a lovely face!

My Lady Wind is grand and strong,
And yet so full of glee,
She almost says, "My little maid,
Come, have a race with me."

COME OUT TO PLAY

Girls and boys, come out to play,
The moon is shining as bright as day:
Leave your supper, and leave your sleep,
And join your playfellows in the street.
Come with a whoop and come with a call,
Come with a good will or not at all.
Up the ladder and down the wall,
A halfpenny roll will serve us all.
You find milk and I 'll find flour,
And we 'll have a pudding in half an hour.

ROMANCE

I saw a ship a-sailing,
    A-sailing on the sea;
Her masts were of the shining gold,
    Her deck of ivory;
And sails of silk, as soft as milk,
    And silvern shrouds had she.

And round about her sailing,
    The sea was sparkling white,
The waves all clapped their hands and sang
    To see so fair a sight.
They kissed her twice, they kissed her thrice,
    And murmured with delight.

11

Then came the gallant captain,
    And stood upon the deck;
In velvet coat, and ruffles white,
    Without a spot or speck;
And diamond rings, and triple strings
    Of pearls around his neck.

And four-and-twenty sailors
    Were round him bowing low;
On every jacket three times three
    Gold buttons in a row;
And cutlasses down to their knees;
    They made a goodly show.

And then the ship went sailing,
    A-sailing o'er the sea;
She dived beyond the setting sun,
    But never back came she,
For she found the lands of the golden sands,
    Where the pearls and diamonds be.
                                    —GABRIEL SETOUN.

SWEET AND LOW

Sweet and low, sweet and low,
    Wind of the western sea,
Low, low, breathe and blow,
    Wind of the western sea!
Over the rolling waters go,
Come from the dying moon and blow,
    Blow him again to me;
While my little one, while my pretty one sleeps.

Sleep and rest, sleep and rest,
    Father will come to thee soon;
Rest, rest, on mother's breast,
    Father will come to thee soon;
Father will come to his babe in the nest;
Silver sails all out of the west,
    Under the silver moon:
Sleep, my little one, sleep, my pretty one, sleep.

—ALFRED TENNYSON.

FOREIGN LANDS

Up into the cherry tree
Who should climb but little me?
I held the trunk with both my hands
And looked abroad on foreign lands.

I saw the next door garden lie,
Adorned with flowers, before my eye,
And many pleasant places more
That I had never seen before.

I saw the dimpling river pass
And be the sky's blue looking-glass;
The dusty roads go up and down
With people tramping in to town.

If I could find a higher tree
Farther and farther I should see,
To where the grown-up river slips
Into the sea among the ships,

To where the roads on either hand
Lead onward into fairyland,
Where all the children dine at five
And all the playthings come alive.
　　　　　　　—ROBERT LOUIS STEVENSON.

14

THE RAGGLE, TAGGLE GYPSIES

There were three gypsies a-come to my door,
    And downstairs ran this lady, O.
One sang high and another sang low,
    And the other sang "Bonnie, Bonnie Biskay, O."

Then she pulled off her silken gown,
    And put on hose of leather, O.
With the ragged, ragged rags about her door
    She 's off with the Raggle, Taggle Gypsies, O.

'T was late last night when my lord came home,
    Inquiring for his lady, O.
The servants said on every hand,
    "She 's gone with the Raggle, Taggle Gypsies, O."

"Oh, saddle for me my milk-white steed,
    Oh, saddle for me my pony, O,
That I may ride and seek my bride
    Who 's gone with the Raggle, Taggle Gypsies, O."

Oh, he rode high and he rode low,
    He rode through woods and copses, O,
Until he came to an open field,
    And there he espied his lady, O.

"What makes you leave your house and lands?
    What makes you leave your money, O?
What makes you leave your new-wedded lord
    To go with the Raggle, Taggle Gypsies, O?"

"What care I for my house and lands?
    What care I for my money, O,
What care I for my new-wedded lord?
    I 'm off with the Raggle, Taggle Gypsies, O."

"Last night you slept on a goose-feather bed,
    With the sheet turned down so bravely, O.
To-night you will sleep in the cold, open field,
    Along with the Raggle, Taggle Gypsies, O."

"What care I for your goose-feather bed,
    With the sheet turned down so bravely, O?
For to-night I shall sleep in a cold, open field,
    Along with the Raggle, Taggle Gypsies, O."

—*Old Folk Song.*

16

FRIENDS

How good to lie a little while
    And look up through the tree!
The Sky is like a kind big smile
    Bent sweetly over me.

The Sunshine flickers through the lace
    Of leaves above my head,
And kisses me upon the face
    Like Mother, before bed.

The Wind comes stealing o'er the grass
    To whisper pretty things,
And though I cannot see him pass,
    I feel his careful wings.

So many gentle Friends are near
    Whom one can scarcely see,
A child should never feel a fear,
    Wherever he may be.
—ABBIE FARWELL BROWN.

THE ROBIN

In the tall elm tree sat the Robin bright,
    Through the rainy April day,
And he caroled clear with a pure delight,
    to the face of the sky so gray.
And the silver rain through the blossoms dropped,
    And fell on the Robin's coat,
And his brave red breast, but he never stopped
    Piping his cheerful note;

For O, the fields were green and glad,
    And the blissful life that stirred
In the earth's wide breast, was full and warm
    In the heart of the little bird.
The rain cloud lifted, the sunset light
    Streamed wide over valley and hill,
As the plains of heaven the land grew bright,
    And the warm south wind was still.

Then loud and clear called the happy bird,
    And rapturously he sang,
Till wood and meadow and river side
    With jubilant echoes rang.
But the sun dropped down in the quiet west,
    And he hushed his song at last;
All nature softly sank to rest
    And the April day had passed.

—CELIA THAXTER.

WHERE GO THE BOATS?

Dark brown is the river,
Golden is the sand.
It flows along forever,
With trees on every hand.

Green leaves a-floating,
Castles of the foam,
Boats of mine a-boating—
Where will all come home?

On goes the river
And out past the mill,
Away down the valley,
Away down the hill.

Away down the river,
A hundred miles or more,
Other little children
Shall bring my boats ashore.
—ROBERT LOUIS STEVENSON.

TO THE LADYBIRD

Ladybird, ladybird! fly away home!
The fieldmouse has gone to her nest,
The daisies have shut up their sleepy red eyes,
And the bees and birds are at rest.

Ladybird, ladybird! fly away home!
    The glowworm is lighting her lamp,
The dew 's falling fast, and your fine speckled wings
    Will flag with the close clinging damp.

Ladybird, ladybird! fly away home!
    The fairybells tinkle afar!
Make haste, or they 'll catch you, and harness you fast
    With a cobweb to Oberon's car.
                              —CAROLINE BOWLES SOUTHEY.

THE BEE AND THE FLOWER

The bee buzzed up in the heat.
"I am faint for your honey, my sweet."
The flower said, "Take it, my dear,
For now is the spring of the year.
        So come, come!"
            "Hum!"
And the bee buzzed down from the heat.

And the bee buzzed up in the cold
When the flower was withered and old.
"Have you still any honey, my dear?"
She said, "It 's the fall of the year,
        But come, come!"
            "Hum!"
And the bee buzzed off in the cold.
                              —ALFRED TENNYSON.

THE FAIRIES

Up the airy mountain,
    Down the rushy glen,
We dare n't go a-hunting,
    For fear of little men;
Wee folk, good folk,
    Trooping all together;
Green jacket, red cap,
    And white owl's feather!

Down along the rocky shore,
    Some make their home,
They live on crispy pancakes
    Of yellow tide-foam;
Some in the reeds
    Of the black mountain lake,
With frogs for their watchdogs,
    All night awake.

High on the hill top
    The old King sits;
He is now so old and gray
    He 's nigh lost his wits.
With a bridge of white mist
    Columbkill he crosses,
On his stately journeys
    From Slieveleague to Rosses;
Or going up with music
    On cold starry nights,
To sup with the queen
    Of the gay Northern Lights.

They stole little Bridget
    For seven years long;
When she came down again
    Her friends were all gone.
They took her lightly back,
    Between the night and morrow,

They thought that she was fast asleep,
    But she was dead with sorrow.
They have kept her ever since
    Deep within the lake,
On a bed of flag leaves,
    Watching till she wake.

By the craggy hillside,
    Through the mosses bare,
They have planted thorn-trees
    For pleasure here and there.
Is any man so daring
    As dig them up in spite,
He shall find their sharpest thorns
    In his bed at night.

Up the airy mountain,
    Down the rushy glen,
We dare n't go a-hunting
    For fear of little men;
Wee folk, good folk,
    Trooping all together;
Green jacket, red cap,
    And white owl's feather!

—WILLIAM ALLINGHAM.

PRINCE TATTERS

Little Prince Tatters has lost his cap!
    Over the hedge he threw it;
Into the water it fell with a clap—
    Stupid old thing to do it!
Now Mother may sigh and Nurse may fume
    For the gay little cap with its eagle plume.
"One cannot be thinking all day of such matters!
    Trifles are trifles!" says little Prince Tatters.

Little Prince Tatters has lost his coat!
    Playing he did not need it;
"Left it *right there*, by the nanny-goat,
    And nobody ever see'd it!"
Now Mother and Nurse may search till night
    For the new little coat with its buttons bright;
But, "Coat-sleeves or shirt-sleeves, how little it matters!
    Trifles are trifles," says little Prince Tatters.

Little Prince Tatters has LOST HIS BALL!
    Rolled away down the street!
Somebody 'll *have to find it*, that 's all,
    Before he can sleep or eat.
Now raise the neighborhood, quickly, do
    And send for the crier and constable too!
"Trifles are trifles; but serious matters
    They must be *seen* to," says little Prince Tatters.
—LAURA E. RICHARDS.

A SAND CASTLE

The tide is out, and all the strand
    Is glistening in the summer sun;
Let 's build a castle of the sand—
    Oh! will not that be glorious fun?

With walls and outworks wide and steep,
    All round about we 'll dig a moat,
And in the midst shall be the keep,
    Where England's flag may proudly float.

And where a drawbridge ought to be,
    We 'll make a causeway to the shore,
Well paved with stones, for you and me
    To get to land when tempests roar.

We 'll sit within our citadel,
    And watch the tide come o'er the rocks;
But we have built it strong and well;
    It will not fall for common shocks.

The moat may fill, the waves may beat,
    We watch the siege all undismayed,
Because, you know, we can retreat
    Along the causeway we have made.

"Haul down your flag!" "Oh, no!" we shout,
    Our drums and trumpets heard afar—
The castle sinks; but we march out
    With all the honors of the war.

A FRIEND IN THE GARDEN

He is not John the gardener,
    And yet the whole day long
Employs himself most usefully,
    The flower beds among.

He is not Tom the pussy-cat,
    And yet the other day,
With stealthy stride and glistening eye,
    He crept upon his prey.

He is not Dash the dear old dog,
    And yet, perhaps, if you
Took pains with him and petted him,
    You 'd come to love him too.

He 's not a Blackbird, though he chirps,
    And though he once was black;
And now he wears a loose, gray coat,
    All wrinkled on the back.

He 's got a very dirty face,
    And very shining eyes;
He sometimes comes and sits indoors;
    He looks—and p'r'aps is—wise.

But in a sunny flower bed
    He has his fixed abode;
He eats the things that eat my plants—
    He is a friendly TOAD.
        —JULIANA HORATIA EWING.

26

THE WORLD'S MUSIC

The world 's a very happy place,
    Where every child should dance and sing,
And always have a smiling face,
    And never sulk for anything.

I waken when the morning 's come,
    And feel the air and light alive
With strange sweet music like the hum
    Of bees about their busy hive.

The linnets play among the leaves
    At hide-and-seek, and chirp and sing;
While, flashing to and from the eaves,
    The swallows twitter on the wing.

And twigs that shake, and boughs that sway;
    And tall old trees you could not climb;
And winds that come, but cannot stay,
    Are singing gayly all the time.

From dawn to dark the old mill-wheel
    Makes music, going round and round;
And dusty-white with flour and meal,
    The miller whistles to its sound.

The brook that flows beside the mill,
    As happy as a brook can be,
Goes singing its own song until
    It learns the singing of the sea.

For every wave upon the sands
    Sings songs you never tire to hear,
Of laden ships from sunny lands
    Where it is summer all the year.

And if you listen to the rain
    When leaves and birds and bees are dumb,
You hear it pattering on the pane
    Like Andrew beating on his drum.

The coals beneath the kettle croon,
    And clap their hands and dance in glee;
And even the kettle hums a tune
    To tell you when it 's time for tea.

The world is such a happy place,
    That children, whether big or small,
Should always have a smiling face
    And never, never sulk at all.
                  —GABRIEL SETOUN.

A FABLE

The mountain and the squirrel
Had a quarrel,
And the former called the latter "Little Prig."
Bun replied,
"You are doubtless very big;
But all sorts of things and weather
Must be taken in together,

To make up a year
And a sphere.
And I think it no disgrace
To occupy my place.
If I 'm not so large as you,
You are not so small as I,
And not half so spry.
I 'll not deny you make
A very pretty squirrel track;
Talents differ; all is well and wisely put;
If I cannot carry forests on my back,
Neither can you crack a nut."

—RALPH WALDO EMERSON.

HOW THE LEAVES CAME DOWN

I 'll tell you how the leaves came down.
   The great Tree to his children said:
"You 're getting sleepy, Yellow and Brown,
   Yes, very sleepy, little Red;
   It is quite time you went to bed."

"Ah," begged each silly, pouting leaf,
   "Let us a little longer stay;
Dear Father Tree, behold our grief;
   'T is such a very pleasant day,
   We do not want to go away."

So just for one more merry day
　　To the great Tree the leaflets clung,
Frolicked and danced, and had their way,
　　Upon the autumn breezes swung,
　　Whispering, all their sports among:

"Perhaps, the great Tree will forget,
　　And let us stay until the spring,
If we all beg, and coax, and fret."
　　But the great Tree did no such thing;
　　He smiled to hear them whispering.

"Come, children, all to bed!" he cried;
　　And ere the leaves could urge their prayer,
He shook his head, and far and wide,
　　Fluttering and rustling everywhere,
　　Down sped the leaflets through the air.

I saw them; on the ground they lay,
　　Golden and red, a huddled swarm,
Waiting till one from far away,
　　White bedclothes heaped upon her arm,
　　Should come to wrap them safe and warm.

The great bare Tree looked down, and smiled.
　　"Good-night, dear little leaves," he said.
And from below each sleepy child
　　Replied, "Good-night," and murmured,
　　"It is so nice to go to bed!"
　　　　　　　　　　　　　　—SUSAN COOLIDGE.

He smiles to see the eyelids close
Above the happy eyes.

THE SANDMAN

The rosy clouds float overhead,
　　The sun is going down;
And now the sandman's gentle tread,
　　Comes stealing through the town.
"White sand, white sand, sand," he softly cries,
　　And, as he shakes his hand,
Straightway there lies in babies' eyes
　　His gift of shining sand.
Blue eyes, gray eyes, black eyes and brown,
As shuts the rose, they softly close, when he goes
　　through the town.

From shiny beaches far away—
　　Yes, in another land—
He gathers up at break of day
　　His store of shining sand.
No tempests beat that shore remote,
　　No ships may sail away;
His little boat alone may float
　　Within that lovely bay.
Blue eyes, gray eyes, black eyes and brown,
As shuts the rose, they softly close, when he goes
　　through the town.

He smiles to see the eyelids close
　　Above the happy eyes,
And every child right well he knows.
　　Oh! he is very wise!

But if, as he goes through the land,
    A naughty baby cries,
His other hand takes dull gray sand
    To close the wakeful eyes.
Blue eyes, gray eyes, black eyes and brown,
As shuts the rose, they softly close, when he goes
    through the town.

So when you hear the sandman's song
    Sound through the twilight sweet,
Be sure you do not keep him long
    Awaiting on the street.
Lie softly down, dear little head;
    Rest quiet, busy hands,
Till by your bed, his good night said,
    He strews the shining sands.
Blue eyes, gray eyes, black eyes and brown,
As shuts the rose, they softly close, when he goes
    through the town.

—MARGARET VANDEGRIFT.

33

LONDON WIND

The wind blows, the wind blows,
    Over the ocean far,
But oh! it has forgot the waves
    And the Isles where the Penguins are.

The wind blows, the wind blows,
    Over the forest wide,
But oh! it has forgot the shade
    And the dells where the hunted hide.

The wind blows, the wind blows,
    Over the houses high,
The paper whirls in the dusty street
    And the clouds are atoss in the sky.
        —LAURENCE ALMA-TADEMA.

ALADDIN

When I was a beggarly boy,
    And lived in a cellar damp,
I had not a friend nor a toy
    But I had Aladdin's lamp.

When I could not sleep for the cold,
    I had fire enough in my brain,
And builded with roofs of gold,
    My beautiful castles in Spain!

Since then I have toiled day and night,
   I have money and power good store,
But I 'd give all my lamps of silver bright
   For the one that is mine no more.

Take, Fortune, whatever you choose,
   You gave and may snatch again,
I have nothing 't would pain me to lose,
   For I own no more castles in Spain!
                              —JAMES RUSSELL LOWELL.

THE BABIE

Nae shoon to hide her tiny taes,
Nae stockings on her feet;
Her supple ankles white as snow,
Or early blossoms sweet.

Her simple dress of sprinkled pink
Her double, dimpled chin;
Her pucker'd lip and bonny mou',
With nae ane tooth between.

Her een sae like her mither's een,
Twa gentle, liquid things;
Her face is like an angel's face—
We 're glad she has nae wings.
                              —HUGH MILLER.

THE GREAT BROWN OWL

The brown Owl sits in the ivy bush,
    And she looketh wondrous wise,
With a horny beak beneath her cowl,
    And a pair of large round eyes.

She sat all day on the self-same spray,
    From sunrise till sunset;
And the dim, gray light it was all too bright
    For the Owl to see in yet.

Jenny-Owlet, Jenny-Owlet, said a merry little bird,
    They say you 're wondrous wise:
But I don't think you see, though you 're looking at ME
    With your large, round, shining eyes.

But night came soon, and the pale white moon
    Rolled high up in the skies;
And the great brown Owl flew away in her cowl,
    With her round large shining eyes.
—MRS. ANN HAWKSHAW.

DAYBREAK

A wind came up out of the sea,
And said, "O mists, make room for me."
It hailed the ships, and cried, "Sail on,
Ye mariners, the night is gone."

And hurried landward far away,
Crying, "Awake, it is the day."
It said to the forest, "Shout!
Hang all your leafy banners out."
It touched the wood bird's folded wing,
And said, "O bird, awake and sing."
—HENRY WADSWORTH LONGFELLOW.

A BIRD'S EXPERIENCE

I lived first in a little house
    And lived there very well;
The world to me was small and round,
    And made of pale blue shell.

I lived next in a little nest,
    Nor needed any other;
I thought the world was made of straw,
    And brooded by my mother.

One day I fluttered from my home
    To see what I could find;
I said, "The world is made of leaves,
    I have been very blind."

At last I flew beyond the nest
    Quite fit for grown-up labors;
I don't know how the world is made,
    And neither do my neighbors.

A BOY'S SONG

Where the pools are bright and deep,
Where the gray trout lies asleep,
Up the river and over the lea,
That 's the way for Billy and me.

Where the blackbird sings the latest,
Where the hawthorn blooms the sweetest,
Where the nestlings chirp and flee,
That 's the way for Billy and me.

Where the mowers mow the cleanest,
Where the hay lies thick and greenest,
There to track the homeward bee,
That 's the way for Billy and me.

Where the hazel bank is steepest,
Where the shadow falls the deepest,
Where the clustering nuts fall free,
That 's the way for Billy and me.

Why the boys should drive away
Little sweet maidens from the play,
Or love to banter and fight so well,
That 's the thing I never could tell.

But this I know, I love to play
Through the meadow, among the hay;
Up the water and o'er the lea,
That 's the way for Billy and me.

—JAMES HOGG.

PIPPA'S SONG

The year 's at the spring
And day 's at the morn;
Morning 's at seven;
The hillside 's dew-pearled;
The lark 's on the wing;
The snail 's on the thorn;
God 's in His heaven—
All 's right with the world!
—ROBERT BROWNING.

THE GRAY DOVES' ANSWER

The leaves were reddening to their fall.
    "Coo!" said the gray doves, "coo!"
As they sunned themselves on the garden wall,
    And the swallows round them flew,
"Whither away, sweet swallows?
    Coo!" said the gray doves, "coo!"
"Far from this land of ice and snow
    To a sunny southern clime we go,
Where the sky is warm and bright and gay:
    Come with us, away, away!

"Come," they said, "to that sunny clime!"
    "Coo!" said the gray doves, "coo!"
"You will die in this land of mist and rime,
    Where 't is bleak the winter through.

Come away!" said the swallows.
   "Coo!" said the gray doves, "coo!
Oh, God in heaven," they said, "is good;
   And little hands will give us food,
And guard us all the winter through.
   Coo!" said the gray doves, "coo!"

APRIL RAIN

It is n't raining rain to me,
   It 's raining daffodils;
In every dimpled drop I see
   Wild flowers on the hills.
The clouds of gray engulf the day,
   And overwhelm the town;
It is n't raining rain to me,
   It 's raining roses down.

It is n't raining rain to me,
   But fields of clover bloom,
Where any buccaneering bee
   May find a bed and room.
A health unto the happy,
   A fig for him who frets—
It is n't raining rain to me,
   It 's raining violets.
                    —ROBERT LOVEMAN.

40

THE SEA PRINCESS

In a palace of pearl and seaweed,
　　Set around with shining shells,
Under the deeps of the ocean,
　　The little sea princess dwells.

Sometimes she sees the shadow
　　Of a great whale passing by,
Or a white-winged vessel sailing
　　Between the sea and sky.

And when through the waves she rises,
　　Beyond the breakers' roar
She hears the shouts of the children
　　At play on the sandy shore;

And sees the ships' sides tower
　　Above like a wet black wall;
Or shouts to the roaring breakers,
　　And answers the sea gull's call.

But down in the quiet waters
　　Better she loves to play,
Making a seaweed garden,
　　Purple and green and gray;

Better she loves to play.
Making a seaweed garden.

Stringing with pearls a necklace,
        Or learning curious spells
From the water witch, gray and ancient,
        And hearing the tales she tells.

Out in the stable her sea horse
        Champs in his crystal stall,
And fishes with scales that glisten
        Come leaping forth at her call.

So the little princess
        Is busy and happy all day
Just as the human children
        Are busy and happy at play.

And when the darkness gathers
        Over the lonely deep,
On a bed of velvet seaweed
        The princess is rocked to sleep.

QUEEN MAB

A little fairy comes at night,
    Her eyes are blue, her hair is brown,
With silver spots upon her wings,
    And from the moon she flutters down.

She has a little silver wand,
    And when a good child goes to bed
She waves her wand from right to left,
    And makes a circle round its head.

And then it dreams of pleasant things,
    Of fountains filled with fairy fish,
And trees that bear delicious fruit,
    And bow their branches at a wish:

Of arbors filled with dainty scents
    From lovely flowers that never fade;
Bright flies that glitter in the sun,
    And glow-worms shining in the shade,

And talking birds with gifted tongues,
    For singing songs and telling tales,
And pretty dwarfs to show the way
    Through fairy hills and fairy dales.

But when a bad child goes to bed,
    From left to right she weaves her rings,

And then it dreams all through the night
    Of only ugly horrid things!

Then lions come with glaring eyes,
    And tigers growl, a dreadful noise,
And ogres draw their cruel knives,
    To shed the blood of girls and boys.

Then stormy waves rush on to drown,
    Or raging flames come scorching round;
Fierce dragons hover in the air,
    And serpents crawl along the ground.

Then wicked children wake and weep,
    And wish the long black gloom away;
But good ones love the dark, and find
    The night as pleasant as the day.
                        —THOMAS HOOD.

THE FAIRY THRALL

On gossamer nights when the moon is low,
    And stars in the mist are hiding,
Over the hill where the foxgloves grow
    You may see the fairies riding.
        Kling! Klang! Kling!
Their stirrups and their bridles ring,
    And their horns are loud and their bugles blow,
When the moon is low.

THE LAMB

Little lamb, who made thee?
Dost thou know who made thee,
Gave thee life, and bade thee feed
By the stream and o'er the mead;
Gave thee clothing of delight,
Softest clothing, woolly, bright;
Gave thee such a tender voice,
Making all the vales rejoice?
    Little lamb, who made thee?
    Dost thou know who made thee?

Little lamb, I 'll tell thee;
Little lamb, I 'll tell thee:
He is called by thy name,
For He calls Himself a Lamb.
He is meek, and He is mild;
He became a little child.
I a child, and thou a lamb,
We are called by His name.
    Little lamb, God bless thee!
    Little lamb, God bless thee!
        —WILLIAM BLAKE.

GOLDEN-ROD

Spring is the morning of the year,
    And summer is the noontide bright;
The autumn is the evening clear
    That comes before the winter's night.

And in the evening, everywhere
    Along the roadside, up and down,
I see the golden torches flare
    Like lighted street lamps in the town.

I think the butterfly and bee,
    From distant meadows coming back,
Are quite contented when they see
    These lamps along the homeward track.

But those who stay too late get lost;
    For when the darkness falls about,
Down every lighted street the Frost
    Will go and put the torches out!
                —Frank Dempster Sherman.

THE QUEST

There once was a restless boy
Who dwelt in a home by the sea,
Where the water danced for joy,
And the wind was glad and free:
But he said, "Good mother, oh! let me go;
For the dullest place in the world, I know,
Is this little brown house,
This old brown house,
Under the apple tree.

"I will travel east and west;
The loveliest homes I 'll see;

48

And when I have found the best,
　Dear mother, I 'll come for thee.
I 'll come for thee in a year and a day,
And joyfully then we 'll haste away,
　　From this little brown house,
　　This old brown house,
　　Under the apple tree."

So he traveled here and there,
　But never content was he,
Though he saw in lands most fair
　The costliest homes there be.
He something missed from the sea or sky,
Till he turned again with a wistful sigh
　　To the little brown house,
　　The old brown house,
　　Under the apple tree.

Then the mother saw and smiled,
　While her heart grew glad and free.
"Hast thou chosen a home, my child?
　Ah, where shall we dwell?" quoth she.
And he said, "Sweet mother, from east to west,
The loveliest home, and the dearest and best,
　　Is a little brown house,
　　An old brown house,
　　Under an apple tree."
　　　　　　　　　　—EUDORA BUMSTEAD.

A GOOD THANKSGIVING

Said Old Gentleman Gay, "On a Thanksgiving Day,
If you want a good time, then give something away."
So he sent a fat turkey to Shoemaker Price,
And the shoemaker said, "What a big bird! how nice!
And since a good dinner 's before me, I ought
To give poor Widow Lee the small chicken I bought."

"This fine chicken, oh, see!" said the pleased Widow Lee,
"And the kindness that sent it, how precious to me!
I would like to make some one as happy as I—
I 'll give Washerwoman Biddy my big pumpkin pie."

"And oh, sure," Biddy said, " 't is the queen of all pies!
Just to look at its yellow face gladdens my eyes.
Now it 's my turn, I think; and a sweet ginger cake
For the motherless Finigan children I 'll bake."

"A sweet cake, all our own! 'T is too good to be true!"
Said the Finigan children, Rose, Denny, and Hugh;
"It smells sweet of spice, and we 'll carry a slice
To poor little Lame Jake—who has nothing that 's nice."

"Oh, I thank you, and thank you!" said little Lame Jake;
"Oh, what beautiful, beautiful, beautiful cake!
And oh, such a big slice! I will save all the crumbs,
And will give 'em to each little sparrow that comes!"
And the sparrows they twittered as if they would say,
Like Old Gentleman Gay, "On a Thanksgiving Day,
If you want a good time, then give something away."
                                        —MARIAN DOUGLAS.

THE LAND OF STORYBOOKS

At evening when the lamp is lit,
Around the fire my parents sit;
They sit at home and talk and sing,
And do not play at anything.

Now, with my little gun, I crawl
All in the dark along the wall,
And follow round the forest track
Away behind the sofa back.

There, in the night, where none can spy,
All in my hunter's camp I lie,
And play at books that I have read
Till it is time to go to bed.

I see the others far away
As if in firelit camp they lay,
And I, like to an Indian scout,
Around their party prowled about.

So, when my nurse comes in for me,
Home I return across the sea,
And go to bed with backward looks
At my dear Land of Storybooks.

—ROBERT LOUIS STEVENSON.

THE CHRISTMAS TREE IN THE NURSERY

With wild surprise
Four great eyes
In two small heads
From neighboring beds
Looked out—and winked—
And glittered and blinked
At a very queer sight
In the dim dawn-light.

As plain as can be
A fairy tree
Flashes and glimmers
And shakes and shimmers.
Red, green, and blue
Meet their view;
Silver and gold
Sharp eyes behold;
Small moons, big stars;
And jams in jars,
And cakes and honey

And thimbles, and money,
Pink dogs, blue cats,
Little squeaking rats,
And candles, and dolls,
And crackers and polls,
A real bird that sings,
And tokens and favors,
And all sorts of things
For the little shavers.

Four black eyes
Grow big with surprise;
And then grow bigger
When a tiny figure,
Jaunty and airy,
A fairy! a fairy!
From the treetop cries:
"Open wide! Black Eyes!
Come, children, wake now!
Your joys you may take now."

Quick as you can think,
Twenty small toes
In four pretty rows,
Like little piggies pink,
All kick in the air—
And before you can wink
The tree stands bare!
—RICHARD WATSON GILDER.

THE WILLOW MAN

There once was a Willow, and he was very old,
And all his leaves fell off from him, and left him in the
      cold;
But ere the rude winter could buffet him with snow,
There grew upon his hoary head a crop of Mistletoe.

All wrinkled and furrowed was this old Willow's skin,
His taper fingers trembled, and his arms were very thin;
Two round eyes and hollow, that stared but did not see,
And sprawling feet that never walked, had this most
      ancient tree.

A Dame who dwelt a-near was the only one who knew
That every year upon his head the Christmas berries grew;
And when the Dame cut them, she said—it was her
      whim—
"A merry Christmas to you, Sir!" *and left a bit for him.*

"Oh, Granny dear, tell us," the children cried, "where we
May find the shining Mistletoe that grows upon the tree?"
At length the Dame told them, but cautioned them to
      mind
To greet the willow civilly, *and leave a bit behind.*

"Who cares," said the children, "for this old Willow man?
We 'll take the Mistletoe, and he may catch us if he can."
With rage the ancient Willow shakes in every limb,
For they have taken all, *and have not left a bit for him.*

Then bright gleamed the holly, the Christmas berries
    shone,
But in the wintry wind without the Willow man did moan:
"Ungrateful, and wasteful! the mystic Mistletoe
A hundred years hath grown on me, but never more shall
    grow."

A year soon passed by, and the children came once more,
But not a sprig of Mistletoe the aged Willow bore.
Each slender spray pointed; he mocked them in his glee,
And chuckled in his wooden heart, that ancient Willow
    tree.

MORAL

O children, who gather the spoils of wood and wold,
From selfish greed and willful waste your little hands
    withhold.
Though fair things be common, this moral bear in mind,
"Pick thankfully and modestly, *and leave a bit behind.*"
—JULIANA HORATIA EWING.

HERE WE COME A-WHISTLING

Here we come a-whistling through the fields so green,
Here we come a-singing, so fair to be seen.
God send you happy, God send you happy,
Pray God send you a Happy New Year.

The roads are very dirty, my boots are very thin,
I have a little pocket to put a penny in.
God send you happy, God send you happy,
Pray God send you a Happy New Year.

Bring out your little table and spread it with a cloth.
Bring out some of your old ale, likewise your Christmas
    loaf.
God send you happy, God send you happy,
Pray God send you a Happy New Year.

God bless the master of this house, likewise the mistress,
    too,
And all the little children that round the table strew.
God send you happy, God send you happy,
Pray God send you a Happy New Year.

SNOW IN TOWN

Nothing is quite so quiet and clean
    As snow that falls in the night;
And is n't it jolly to jump from bed
    And find the whole world white?

It lies on the window ledges,
    It lies on the boughs of the trees,
While sparrows crowd at the kitchen door,
    With a pitiful "If you *please?*"

It lies on the arm of the lamp-post,
    Where the lighter's ladder goes,
And the policeman under it beats his arms,
    And stamps—to feel his toes;

The butcher's boy is rolling a ball
    To throw at the man with coals,
And old Mrs. Ingram has fastened a piece
    Of flannel under her soles;

No sound there is in the snowy road
    From the horses' cautious feet,
And all is hushed but the postman's knocks
    Rat-tatting down the street,

Till men come round with shovels
    To clear the snow away,—
What a pity it is that when it falls
    They never let it stay!

And while we are having breakfast
    Papa says, "Is n't it light?
And all because of the thousands of geese
    The Old Woman plucked last night.

"And if you are good," he tells us,
    "And attend to your A B C,
You may go in the garden and make a snow man
    As big or bigger than me."
                                    —RICKMAN MARK.

THE NEW YEAR

Ring out, wild bells, to the wild sky,
    The flying cloud, the frosty light;
    The year is dying in the night;
Ring out, wild bells, and let him die.

Ring out the old, ring in the new,
    Ring, happy bells, across the snow:
    The year is going, let him go;
Ring out the false, ring in the true.
                                    —ALFRED TENNYSON.

59

A TRAGIC STORY

There lived a sage in days of yore,
And he a handsome pigtail wore;
But wondered much, and sorrowed more,
Because it hung behind him.

He mused upon the curious case,
And swore he 'd change the pigtail's place,
And have it hanging at his face,
Not dangling there behind him.

Says he, "The mystery I 've found,—
I 'll turn me round,"—he turned him round;
But still it hung behind him.

Then round and round, and out and in,
All day the puzzled sage did spin;
In vain—it mattered not a pin,—
The pigtail hung behind him.

And right, and left, and round about,
And up, and down, and in, and out
He turned; but still the pigtail stout
Hung steadily behind him.

And though his efforts never slack,
And though he twist, and twirl, and tack,
Alas! still faithful to his back,
The pigtail hangs behind him.

—ALBERT VON CHAMISSO.

(Translated by William Makepeace Thackeray.)

THE WIND AND THE MOON

Said the Wind to the Moon, "I will blow you out.
      You stare
      In the air
      Like a ghost in a chair,
Always looking what I am about—
I hate to be watched; I 'll blow you out."

The Wind blew hard, and out went the Moon.
      So, deep
      On a heap
      Of clouds to sleep,
Down lay the Wind, and slumbered soon,
Muttering low, "I 've done for *that* Moon."

He turned in his bed; she was there again!
      On high
      In the sky,
      With her one ghost eye,
The Moon shone white and alive and plain.
Said the Wind, "I will blow you out again."

The Wind blew hard, and the Moon grew dim.
>   "With my sledge
>   And my wedge,
>   I have knocked off her edge!
If only I blow right fierce and grim,
The creature will soon be dimmer than dim."

He blew and he blew, and she thinned to a thread.
>   "One puff
>   More 's enough
>   To blow her to snuff!
One good puff more where the last was bred,
And glimmer, glimmer, glum will go the thread."

He blew a great blast, and the thread was gone.
>   In the air
>   Nowhere
>   Was a moonbeam bare;
Far off and harmless the shy stars shone—
Sure and certain the Moon was gone!

The Wind he took to his revels once more;
>   On down
>   In town,
>   Like a merry-mad clown,
He leaped and hallooed with whistle and roar—
"What 's that?" The glimmering thread once more!

He flew in a rage—he danced and blew;
     But in vain
     Was the pain
     Of his bursting brain;
For still the broader the Moon-scrap grew,
The broader he swelled his big cheeks and blew.

Slowly she grew—till she filled the night,
     And shone
     On her throne
     In the sky alone,
A matchless, wonderful silvery light,
Radiant and lovely, the Queen of the Night.

Said the Wind: "What a marvel of power am I!
     With my breath,
     Good faith!
     I blew her to death—
First blew her away right out of the sky—
Then blew her in; what strength have I!"

But the Moon she knew nothing about the affair;
     For, high
     In the sky,
     With her one white eye,
Motionless, miles above the air,
She had never heard the great Wind blare.

—GEORGE MACDONALD.

A SAD LITTLE LASS

"Why sit you here, my lass?" said he.
"I came to see the king," said she,—
"To see the king come riding by,
While all the eager people cry,
'God bless the king, and long live he!'
And therefore sit I here," said she.

"Why do you weep, my lass?" said he.
"Because that I am sad," said she.
"For when the king came riding by,
And all the people raised a cry,
I was so small I could not see;
And therefore do I weep," said she.

"Then weep no more, my lass," said he.
"And pray, good sir, why not?" said she.
"Lift up your eyes of bonnie blue,
And look and look me through and through;
Nor say the king you could not see.
I am the king, my lass," said he.

      —MARGARET JOHNSON.

CHANTICLEER

I wake! I feel the day is near;
    I hear the red cock crowing!
He cries " 'T is dawn!" How sweet and clear
His cheerful call comes to my ear,
    While light is slowly growing.

The white snow gathers, flake on flake;
    I hear the red cock crowing!
Is anybody else awake
To see the winter morning break,
    While thick and fast 't is snowing?

I think the world is all asleep;
    I hear the red cock crowing!
Out of the frosty pane I peep;
The drifts are piled so wide and deep,
    And the wild wind is blowing!

Nothing I see has shape or form;
    I hear the red cock crowing!
But that dear voice comes through the storm
To greet me in my nest so warm,
    As if the sky were glowing!

A happy little child, I lie
    And hear the red cock crowing.
The day is dark. I wonder why
His voice rings out so brave and high,
    With gladness overflowing.

—CELIA THAXTER.

LITTLE BUD DANDELION

Little Bud Dandelion
Hears from her nest
"Merry Heart, Starry Eyes,
Wake from your rest."
Wide ope the daisy lids
Robin 's above,
Wise little Dandelion
Smiles at his love.

Gay little Dandelion
Lights up the meads,
Swings on her slender foot,
Telleth her beads,
Lists to the robin's note
Poured from above;
Wise little Dandelion
Asks not for love.

Cold lie the daisy banks
Clothed but in green,
Where, in the days agone,
Bright hues were seen.
Wild pinks are slumbering,
Violets delay;
True little Dandelion
Greeteth the May.

Brave little Dandelion!
Fast falls the snow,
Bending the daffodil's
Haughty head low.
Under that fleecy tent
Careless of cold,
Blithe little Dandelion
Counteth her gold.

Meek little Dandelion,
Groweth more fair
Till dies the amber dew
Out from her hair.
High rides the thirsty sun,
Fiercely and high;
Faint little Dandelion
Closeth her eye.

Pale little Dandelion,
In her white shroud,
Heareth the angel-breeze
Call from the cloud;
Tiny plumes fluttering
Make no delay;
Little winged Dandelion
Soareth away.

—HELEN BARRON BOSTWICK.

THE FAIRIES' SHOPPING

Where do you think the Fairies go
To buy their blankets ere the snow?

When Autumn comes, with frosty days,
The sorry, shivering little Fays

Begin to think it 's time to creep
Down to their caves for Winter sleep.

But first they come from far and near
To buy, where shops are not too dear.

(The wind and frost bring prices down
So Fall 's their time to come to town!)

Where on the hillside rough and steep
Browse all day long the cows and sheep,

The mullein's yellow candles burn
Over the heads of dry sweet fern:

All summer long the mullein weaves
His soft and thick and woolly leaves.

Warmer blankets were never seen
Than these broad leaves of fuzzy green.

(The cost of each is but a shekel
Made from the gold of honeysuckle!)

To buy their sheets and fine white lace
With which to trim a pillow case,

They only have to go next door,
Where stands a sleek brown spider's store,

And there they find the misty threads
Ready to cut into sheet and spreads;

Then, for a pillow, pluck with care
Some soft-winged seeds as light as air;

Just what they want the thistle brings,
But thistles are such surly things—

And so, though it is somewhat high,
The clematis the Fairies buy.

The only bedsteads that they need
Are silky pods of ripe milk-weed,

With hangings of the dearest things—
Autumn leaves, or butterflies' wings!

And dandelions' fuzzy heads
They use to stuff their feather beds;

And yellow snapdragons supply
The nightcaps that the Fairies buy,

To which some blades of grass they pin,
And tie them 'neath each little chin.

Then, shopping done, the Fairies cry,
"Our Summer 's gone! Oh, sweet, good-by!"

And sadly to their caves they go,
To hide away from Winter's snow—

And then, though winds and storms may beat,
The Fairies' sleep is warm and sweet!
                              —MARGARET DELAND.

THE CATERPILLAR

A tired caterpillar went to sleep one day
In a snug little cradle of silken gray.
And he said, as he softly curled up in his nest,
"Oh, crawling was pleasant, but rest is best."

He slept through the winter long and cold,
All tightly up in his blanket rolled,
And at last he awoke on a warm spring day
To find that winter had gone away.

He woke to find he had golden wings,
And no longer need crawl over sticks and things.
"Oh, the earth is nice," said the glad butterfly,
"But the sky is best, when we learn to fly."

THE OWL AND THE PUSSY-CAT

The Owl and the Pussy-Cat went to sea
    In a beautiful pea-green boat:
They took some honey, and plenty of money
    Wrapped up in a five-pound note.
The Owl looked up to the stars above,
    And sang to a small guitar,
"O lovely Pussy, O Pussy, my love,
    What a beautiful Pussy you are,—you are!
    What a beautiful Pussy you are!"

Pussy said to the Owl, "You elegant fowl,
    How charmingly sweet you sing!
Oh! let us be married, too long we have tarried,
    But what shall we do for a ring?"
They sailed away, for a year and a day
    To the land where the bong-tree grows;
And there in a wood a Piggy-wig stood
    With a ring at the end of his nose,—his nose,
    With a ring at the end of his nose.

"Dear Pig, are you willing to sell for one shilling
    Your ring?" Said the Piggy, "I will."
So they took it away, and were married next day
    By the Turkey who lives on the hill.
They dined on mince and slices of quince,
    Which they ate with a runcible spoon;
And hand in hand, on the edge of the sand
    They danced by the light of the moon,—the moon,
    They danced by the light of the moon.
                              —EDWARD LEAR.

READY FOR DUTY

Daffy-down-dilly came up in the cold,
    Through the brown mold.
Although the March breezes blew keen on her face,
Although the white snow lay on many a place.

Daffy-down-dilly had heard under ground
    The sweet rushing sound
Of the streams, as they burst off their white winter
    chains—
Of the whistling spring winds and the pattering rains.

"Now then," thought Daffy, deep down in her heart,
    "It 's time I should start!"
So she pushed her soft leaves through the hard frozen
    ground,
Quite up to the surface, and then she looked round.

There was snow all about her—gray clouds overhead,
    The trees all looked dead.
Then how do you think Daffy-down-dilly felt,
When the sun would not shine and the ice would not
    melt?

"Cold weather!" thought Daffy, still working away
    "The earth 's hard to-day!
There 's but a half inch of my leaves to be seen,
And two-thirds of that is more yellow than green."

"I can't do much yet—but I 'll do what I can.
   It 's well I began!
For unless I can manage to lift up my head,
The people will think that the Spring herself 's dead."

So, little by little, she brought her leaves out,
   All clustered about;
And then her bright flowers began to unfold,
Till Daffy stood robed in her spring green and gold.

O Daffy-down-dilly! so brave and so true!
   I wish all were like you!
So ready for duty in all sorts of weather,
And holding forth courage and beauty together.

—ANNA B. WARNER.

HARK! HARK! THE LARK

Hark! hark! the lark at heaven's gate sings,
    And Phœbus 'gins arise
His steeds to water at those springs
    On chaliced flowers that lies;
And winking Mary-buds begin to ope their golden eyes;
With everything that pretty is, my lady sweet, arise;
Arise, arise.

—WILLIAM SHAKESPEARE.

UNDER THE GREENWOOD TREE

Under the greenwood tree,
Who loves to lie with me,
And tune his merry note
Unto the sweet bird's throat—
Come hither, come hither, come hither:
Here shall he see
No enemy
But winter and rough weather.

Who doth ambition shun,
And loves to lie i' the sun,
Seeking the food he eats,
And pleased with what he gets,
Come hither, come hither, come hither:
Here shall he see
No enemy
But winter and rough weather.

—WILLIAM SHAKESPEARE.

DISCONTENT

Down in a field, one day in June,
    The flowers all bloomed together,
Save one, who tried to hide herself,
    And drooped, that pleasant weather.

A robin, who had flown too high
    And felt a little lazy,
Was resting near a buttercup,
    Who wished she were a daisy.

For daisies grow so trim and tall;
    She always had a passion
For wearing frills around her neck,
    In just the daisies' fashion.

And buttercups must always be
    The same old, tiresome color,
While daisies dress in gold and white,
    Although their gold is duller.

"Dear robin," said the sad young flower,
    "Perhaps you 'd not mind trying
To find a nice white frill for me
    Some day, when you are flying."

"You silly thing!" the robin said,
  "I think you must be crazy:
I 'd rather be my honest self,
  Than any made-up daisy.

"You 're nicer in your own bright gown;
  The little children love you:
Be the best buttercup you can,
  And think no flower above you.

"Though swallows leave me out of sight,
  We 'd better keep our places:
Perhaps the world would all go wrong
  With one too many daisies.

"Look bravely up into the sky,
  And be content with knowing
That God wished for a buttercup
  Just here, where you are growing."
                    —SARAH ORNE JEWETT.

MINE HOST OF "THE GOLDEN APPLE"

A goodly host one day was mine,
A Golden Apple his only sign,
That hung from a long branch, ripe and fine.
My host was the bountiful apple tree;
He gave me shelter and nourished me
With the best of fare, all fresh and free.

And light-winged guests came not a few,
To his leafy inn, and sipped the dew,
And sang their best songs ere they flew.

I slept at night, on a downy bed
Of moss, and my Host benignly spread
His own cool shadow over my head.
When I asked what reckoning there might be,
He shook his broad boughs cheerily:—
A blessing be thine, green Apple tree!
—THOMAS WESTWOOD.

MARGERY BROWN

"Margery Brown on the top of the hill,
    Why are you standing idle still?"
"Oh, I 'm looking over to London town;
    Shall I see the horsemen if I go down?"

"Margery Brown on the top of the hill,
    Why are you standing listening still?"
"Oh, I hear the bells of London ring,
    And I hear the men and maidens sing."

"Margery Brown on the top of the hill,
    Why are you standing, waiting still?"
"Oh, a knight is there, but I can't go down,
    For the bells ring strangely in London town."
—KATE GREENAWAY.

THE DUMB SOLDIER

When the grass was closely mown,
Walking on the lawn alone,
In the turf a hole I found,
And hid a soldier underground.

Spring and daisies come apace;
Grasses hide my hiding place;
Grasses run like a green sea
O'er the lawn up to my knee.

Under grass alone he lies,
Looking up with leaden eyes,
Scarlet coat and pointed gun,
To the stars and to the sun.

When the grass is ripe like grain,
When the scythe is stoned again,
When the lawn is shaven clear,
Then my hole shall reappear.

I shall find him, never fear,
I shall find my grenadier;
But for all that 's gone and come,
I shall find my soldier dumb.

He has lived, a little thing,
In the grassy woods of spring;
Done, if he could tell me true,
Just as I should like to do.

He has seen the starry hours
And the springing of the flowers;
And the fairy things that pass
In the forests of the grass.

In the silence he has heard
Talking bee and ladybird,
And the butterfly has flown
O'er him as he lay alone.

Not a word will he disclose,
Not a word of all he knows.
I must lay him on the shelf,
And make up the tale myself.

—ROBERT LOUIS STEVENSON.

BIG SMITH

Are you a Giant, great big man, or is your real name
    Smith?
Nurse says—you 've got a hammer that you hit bad
    children with.
I 'm good to-day, and so I 've come to see if it is true
That you can turn a red-hot rod into a horse's shoe.

Why do you make the horses' shoes of iron instead of
    leather?
Is it because they are allowed to go out in bad weather?
If horses should be shod with iron, Big Smith, will you
    shoe mine?
For now I may not take him out, excepting when it 's fine.

Although he 's not a real live horse, I 'm very fond of him;
His harness won't take off and on, but still it 's new and
    trim.
His tail is hair; he has four legs, but neither hoofs nor
    heels:
I think he 'd seem more like a horse without those yellow
    wheels.

If horses should be shod with iron
Big Smith, will you shoe mine?

They say that Dapple-gray 's not yours, but don't you wish
    he were?
My horse's coat is only paint, but his is soft gray hair;
His face is big and kind like yours, his forelock white as
    snow—
Shan't you be sorry when you 've done his shoes and he
    must go?

I do so wish, Big Smith, that I might come and live with
    you—
To rake the fire, to heat the rods, to hammer two and two.
To be so black, and not to have to wash unless I choose;
To pat the dear old horses, and to mend their poor old
    shoes.

When all the world is dark at night, you work among the
    stars,
A shining shower of fireworks beat out of red-hot bars.
I 've seen you beat, I 've heard you sing, when I was going
    to bed;
And now your face and arms looked black, and now were
    glowing red.

The more you work, the more you sing, the more the
   bellows roar;
The falling stars, the flying sparks stream shining more and
   more.
You hit so hard, you look so hot, and yet you never tire;
It must be very nice to be allowed to play with fire.

I long to beat and sing and shine, as you do, but instead
I put away my horse, and Nurse puts me away to bed.
I wonder if you go to bed; I often think I 'll keep
Awake and see, but, though I try, I always fall asleep.

I know it 's very silly, but I sometimes am afraid
Of being in the dark alone, especially in bed,
But when I see your forge-light come and go upon the
   wall,
And hear you through the window, I am not afraid at all.

I often hear a trotting horse, I sometimes hear it stop;
I hold my breath—you stay your song—it 's at the
   blacksmith's shop.
Before it goes, I 'm apt to fall asleep, Big Smith, it 's true;
But then I dream of hammering that horse's shoes
   with you!

—JULIANA HORATIA EWING.

REMORSE

I killed a robin. The little thing,
With scarlet breast and glossy wing,
That comes on the apple tree to sing.

I flung a stone as he twittered there,
I only meant to give him a scare,
But off it went—and hit him square.

A little flutter—a little cry—
Then on the ground I saw him lie,
I did n't think he was going to die.

But as I watched him I soon could see
He never would sing for you or me
Any more in the apple tree.

Never more in the morning light,
Never more in the sunshine bright,
Trilling his song in gay delight.

And I 'm thinking every summer day,
How never, never can I repay
The little life I took away.

—SYDNEY DAYRE.

FAREWELL TO THE FARM

The coach is at the door at last,
The eager children mounting fast
And kissing hands, in chorus sing;
"Good-by, Good-by to everything!"

To house and garden, field and lawn,
The meadow gates we swang upon,
To pump and stable, tree and swing,
"Good-by, Good-by to everything!"

And fare you well, forever more,
A ladder at the hayloft door,
O hayloft where the cobwebs cling,
"Good-by, Good-by to everything."

Crack goes the whip and off we go,
The trees and houses smaller grow,
Last, round the woody turn we swing,
"Good-by, Good-by, to everything."
—ROBERT LOUIS STEVENSON.

LITTLE SORROW

Among the thistles on the hill,
    In tears, sat little Sorrow;
"I see a black cloud in the west,
    'T will bring a storm to-morrow.
And when it storms, where shall I be?
    And what will keep the rain from me?
Woe 's me!" said little Sorrow.

"But now the air is soft and sweet,
    The sun is bright," said Pleasure;
"Here is my pipe,—if you will dance,
    I 'll wake my merriest measure;
Or, if you choose, we 'll sit beneath
    The red rose tree, and twine a wreath;
Come, come with me!" said Pleasure.

"O, I want neither dance nor flowers,—
    They 're not for me," said Sorrow,
"When that black cloud is in the west,
    And it will storm to-morrow!
And if it storm what shall I do?
    I have no heart to play with you,—
Go! go!" said little Sorrow.

But lo! when came the morrow's morn,
    The clouds were all blown over;
The lark sprang singing from his nest
    Among the dewy clover;

And Pleasure called, "Come out and dance!
　　To-day you mourn no evil chance;
The clouds have all blown over!"

"And if they have, alas! alas!
　　Poor comfort that!" said Sorrow;
"For if to-day we miss the storm,
　　'T will surely come to-morrow,—
And be the fiercer for delay!
　　I am too sore at heart to play;
Woe 's me!" said little Sorrow.
　　　　　　　　　　—MARIAN DOUGLAS.

FOUR-LEAF CLOVER

I know a place where the sun is like gold,
　　And the cherry blooms burst with snow,
And down underneath is the loveliest nook
　　Where the four-leaf clovers grow.

One leaf is for hope, and one is for faith,
　　And one is for love, you know,
And God put another one in for luck—
　　If you search, you will find where they grow.

But you must have hope, and you must have faith,
　　You must love and be strong—and so—
If you work, if you wait, you will find the place
　　Where the four-leaf clovers grow.

　　　　　　　　　　—ELLA HIGGINSON.

88

THE FOUR PRINCESSES

Four Princesses lived in a Green Tower—
    A bright green tower in the middle of the sea;
And no one could think—oh, no one could think—
    Who the Four Princesses could be.

One looked to the North, and one to the South,
    And one to the East, and one to the West;
They were all so pretty, so very pretty,
    You could not tell which was the prettiest.

Their curls were golden—their eyes were blue,
    And their voices were sweet as a silvery bell;
And four white birds around them flew,
    But where they came from—*who* could tell?

Ah, who could tell? for no one knew,
    And not a word could you hear them say.
But the sound of their singing, like church bells ringing,
    Would sweetly float as they passed away.

For under the sun, and under the stars,
    They often sailed on the distant sea;
There, in their Green Tower and Roses Bower—
    They lived again—a mystery.

—KATE GREENAWAY.

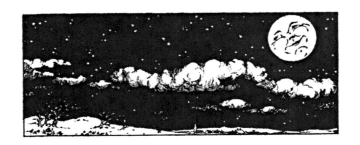

MR. MOON

A SONG OF THE LITTLE PEOPLE

O Moon, Mr. Moon,
When you comin' down?
Down on the hilltop,
Down in the glen,
Out in the clearin',
To play with little men?
Moon, Mr. Moon,
When you comin' down?

O Mr. Moon,
Hurry up your stumps!
Don't you hear Bullfrog
Callin' to his wife,
And old black Cricket
A-wheezin' at his fife?
Hurry up your stumps,
And get on your pumps!
Moon, Mr. Moon,
When you comin' down?

O Mr. Moon,
Hurry up along!
The reeds in the current
Are whisperin' slow;
The river 's a-wimplin'
To and fro.
Hurry up along,
Or you 'll miss the song!
Moon, Mr. Moon,
When you comin' down?

O Mr. Moon,
We 're all here!
Honey-bug, Thistledrift,
White-imp, Weird,
Wryface, Billiken,
Quidnunc, Queered;
We 're all here,
And the coast is clear!
Moon, Mr. Moon,
When you comin' down?

O Mr. Moon,
We 're the little men!
Dewlap, Pussymouse,
Ferntip, Freak,
Drink-again, Shambler,
Talkytalk, Squeak;

Three times ten
Of us little men!
Moon, Mr. Moon,
When you comin' down?

O Mr. Moon,
We 're all ready!
Tallenough, Squaretoes,
Amble, Tip,
Buddybud, Heigho,
Little Black Pip;
We 're all ready,
And the wind walks steady!
Moon, Mr. Moon
When you comin' down?

O Mr. Moon,
We 're thirty score;
Yellowbeard, Piper,
Lieabed, Toots,
Meadowbee, Moonboy,
Bully-in-boots;
Three times more
Than thirty score.
Moon, Mr. Moon,
When you comin' down?

O Mr. Moon,
Keep your eye peeled;
Watch out to windward,
Or you 'll miss the fun,
Down by the acre
Where the wheat-waves run;
Keep your eye peeled
For the open field.
Moon, Mr. Moon,
When you comin' down?

O Mr. Moon,
There 's not much time!
Hurry, if you 're comin',
You lazy old bones!
You can sleep to-morrow
While the Buzbuz drones;
There 's not much time
Till the church bells chime.
Moon, Mr. Moon,
When you comin' down?

O Mr. Moon,
Just see the clover!
Soon we 'll be going
Where the Gray Goose went
When all her money
Was spent, spent, spent!

Down through the clover,
When the revel 's over!
Moon, Mr. Moon,
When you comin' down?

O Moon, Mr. Moon,
When you comin' down?
Down where the Good Folk
Dance in a ring,
Down where the Little Folk
Sing?
Moon, Mr. Moon,
When you comin' down?
—BLISS CARMAN.

JOHN GRUMBLIE

John Grumblie vow'd by the light of the moon,
    And the green leaves on the tree,
That he could do more work in a day
    Than his wife could do in three.
"With all my heart," his wife, Betty, said,
    "If that you will allow,
To-morrow you 'll stay at home in my stead,
    And I 'll go drive the plow."

"But you must milk Tidy, the cow,
    For fear that she go dry;
And you must feed the little pigs
    That are within the sty.
And you must mind the speckled hen,
    For fear she lay away;
And you must reel the spool of yarn
    That I spun yesterday."

The old woman took a staff in her hand,
    And went to drive the plow;
Her husband took a pail in his hand,
    And went to milk the cow.
But Tidy hinched, and Tidy flinched,
    And Tidy broke his nose,
And Tidy gave him such a blow,
    That blood ran down to his toes.

"High, Tidy! ho, Tidy! high, Tidy!
        Tidy, stand thou still;
If ever I milk thee, Tidy, again,
        'T will be sore against my will."
He went to feed the little pigs
        That ran within the sty;
He hit his head against the beam,
        And he made the blood to fly.

He went to mind the speckled hen,
        For fear she 'd lay astray;
And he forgot to reel the yarn
        His wife spun yesterday.
So he swore by the sun, the moon, and the stars,
        And the green leaves on the tree,
If his wife ne'er did a day's work in her life,
        She would ne'er be blamed by he!

        —*Old Rhyme..*

THE WISE FAIRY

Once, in a rough, wild country,
        On the other side of the sea,
There lived a dear little fairy,
        And her home was in a tree;
A dear little, queer little fairy,
        And as rich as she could be.

96

To northward and to southward,
    She could overlook the land,
And that was why she had her house
    In a tree, you understand.
For she was the friend of the friendless,
    And her heart was in her hand.

And when she saw poor women
    Patiently, day by day,
Spinning, spinning, and spinning
    Their lonesome lives away,
She would hide in the flax of their distaffs
    A lump of gold, they say.

And when she saw poor ditchers,
    Knee-deep in some wet dike,
Digging, digging, and digging,
    To their very graves, belike,
She would hide a shining lump of gold
    Where their spades would be sure to strike.

And when she saw poor children
    Their goats from the pastures take,
Or saw them milking and milking,
    Till their arms were ready to break,
What a splashing in their milking-pails
    Her gifts of gold would make!

Sometimes in the night, a fisher
    Would hear her sweet low call,
And all at once a salmon of gold
    Right out of his net would fall;
But what I have to tell you
    Is the strangest thing of all.

If any ditcher, or fisher,
    Or child, or spinner old,
Bought shoes for his feet, or bread to eat,
    Or a coat to keep from the cold,
The gift of the good old fairy
    Was always trusty gold.

But if a ditcher, or fisher,
    Or spinner, or child so gay,
Bought jewels, or wine, or silks so fine,
    Or staked his pleasure at play,
The fairy's gold in his very hold
    Would turn to a lump of clay.

So, by and by the people
    Got open their stupid eyes:
"We must learn to spend to some good end,"
    They said, "if we are wise;
'T is not in the gold we waste or hold,
    That a golden blessing lies."
              —ALICE CARY.

PIGWIGGEN ARMS HIMSELF

He quickly arms him for the field,
A little cockle-shell his shield,
Which he could very bravely wield,
    Yet could it not be pierced:
His spear a bent both stiff and strong,
And well-near of two inches long:
The pile was of a horsefly's tongue,
    Whose sharpness naught reversed.

And puts him on a coat of mail,
Which was of a fish's scale,
That when his foe should him assail,
    No point should be prevailing:
His rapier was a hornet's sting;
It was a very dangerous thing;
For if he chanced to hurt the king,
    It would be long in healing.

His helmet was a beetle's head,
Most horrible and full of dread,
That able was to strike one dead,
    Yet did it well become him.
And for a plume a horse's hair,
Which, being tossed by the air,
Had force to strike his foe with fear,
    And turn his weapon from him.

Himself he on an earwig set,
Yet scarce he on his back could get,
So oft and high he did curvet,
    E'er he himself could settle:
He made him turn, and stop, and bound,
To gallop, and to trot the round,
He scarce could stand on any ground,
    He was so full of mettle.
            —MICHAEL DRAYTON.

THE FAIRY SHOEMAKER

Little cowboy, what have you heard
Up on the lonely rath's green mound!
Only the plaintive yellow bird
Sighing in sultry fields around,
Chary, chary, chary, chee-ee?
Only the grasshopper, and the bee?
      "Tip-tap, rip-rap,
      Tick-a-tack-too!
      Scarlet leather sewn together,
      This will make a shoe,
      Left, right, pull it tight;
      Summer days are warm;
      Underground in winter,
      Laughing at the storm!"

Lay your ear close to the hill.
Do you not catch the tiny clamor,

Busy click of an elfin hammer,
Voice of the Lepracaun singing shrill
As he merrily plies his trade?
      He 's a span
      And a quarter in height.
      Get him in sight, hold him tight,
      And you 're a made Man!

You watch your cattle the summer day,
Sup on potatoes, sleep in the hay:
How would you like to roll in your carriage,
Look for a duchess's daughter in marriage?
Seize the Shoemaker—then you may:
      "Big boots a-hunting,
      Sandals in the hall,
      White for a wedding feast,
      Pink for a ball.
      This way, that way,
      So we make a shoe;
      Getting rich every stitch,
      Tick-tack-too!"
Nine and ninety treasure crocks
This keen miser-fairy hath,
Hid in mountains, woods and rocks,
Ruin and round tower, cave and rath,
And where the cormorants build
      From times of old
      Guarded by him

Each of them filled
Full to the brim with gold!

I caught him at work one day myself,
In the castle ditch, where foxglove grows;
A wrinkled, wizened, and bearded elf,
Spectacles stuck on his pointed nose,
Silver buckles to his hose,
Leather apron, shoe in his lap.
    "Rip-rap, tip-tap,
    Tick-tack-too!
    (A grasshopper on my cap!
    Away the moth flew!)
    Buskins for a fairy prince,
    Brogues for his son;
    Pay me well, pay me well,
    When the job is done!"
The rogue was mine, beyond a doubt;
I stared at him, he stared at me
"Servant, sir!" "Humph!" says he,
And pulled a snuff-box out.
He took a long pinch, looked better pleased,
The queer little Lepracaun;
Offered the box with a dainty grace—
Pouf! he flung the dust in my face!
    And while I sneezed,
      Was gone!
        —WILLIAM ALLINGHAM.

THE WALRUS AND THE CARPENTER

The sun was shining on the sea,
    Shining with all his might:
He did his very best to make
    The billows smooth and bright—
And this was odd, because it was
    The middle of the night.

The moon was shining sulkily,
    Because she thought the sun
Had got no business to be there
    After the day was done—
"It 's very rude of him," she said,
    "To come and spoil the fun!"

The sea was wet as wet could be,
　　The sands were dry as dry.
You could not see a cloud, because
　　No cloud was in the sky:
No birds were flying overhead—
　　There were no birds to fly.

The Walrus and the Carpenter
　　Were walking close at hand:
They wept like anything to see
　　Such quantities of sand:
"If this were only cleared away,"
　　They said, "it would be grand!"

"If seven maids with seven mops
　　Swept it for half a year,
Do you suppose," the Walrus said,
　　"That they could get it clear?"
"I doubt it," said the Carpenter,
　　And shed a bitter tear.

"O Oysters, come and walk with us!"
　　The Walrus did beseech.
"A pleasant walk, a pleasant talk,
　　Along the briny beach:
We cannot do with more than four,
　　To give a hand to each."

The eldest Oyster looked at him,
　　But never a word he said:
The eldest Oyster winked his eye,
　　And shook his heavy head—
Meaning to say he did not choose
　　To leave the oyster-bed.

But four young Oysters hurried up
　　All eager for the treat:
Their coats were brushed, their faces washed,
　　Their shoes were clean and neat—
And this was odd, because, you know,
　　They had n't any feet.

Four other Oysters followed them,
　　And yet another four;
And thick and fast they came at last,
　　And more, and more, and more—
All hopping through the frothy waves,
　　And scrambling to the shore.

The Walrus and the Carpenter
　　Walked on a mile or so,
And then they rested on a rock
　　Conveniently low:
And all the little Oysters stood
　　And waited in a row.

"The time has come," the Walrus said,
    "To talk of many things:
Of shoes—and ships—and sealing-wax—
    Of cabbages—and kings—
And why the sea is boiling hot—
    And whether pigs have wings."

"But wait a bit," the Oysters cried,
    "Before we have our chat;
For some of us are out of breath,
    And all of us are fat!"
"No hurry!" said the Carpenter.
    They thanked him much for that.

"A loaf of bread," the Walrus said,
    "Is what we chiefly need:
Pepper and vinegar besides
    Are very good indeed—
Now, if you 're ready, Oysters dear,
    We can begin to feed."

"But not on us!" the Oysters cried,
    Turning a little blue.
"After such kindness, that would be
    A dismal thing to do!"
"The night is fine," the Walrus said.
    "Do you admire the view?

"It was so kind of you to come!
    And you are very nice!"
The Carpenter said nothing but
    "Cut us another slice:
I wish you were not quite so deaf—
    I 've had to ask you twice!"

"It seems a shame," the Walrus said,
    "To play them such a trick,
After we 've brought them out so far,
    And made them trot so quick!"
The Carpenter said nothing but
    "The butter 's spread too thick!"

"I weep for you," the Walrus said:
    "I deeply sympathize."
With sobs and tears he sorted out
    Those of the largest size,
Holding his pocket handkerchief
    Before his streaming eyes.

"O Oysters," said the Carpenter,
    "You 've had a pleasant run
Shall we be trotting home again?"
    But answer came there none—
And this was scarcely odd, because
    They 'd eaten every one.
                        —LEWIS CARROLL.

107

THE FAIRIES OF THE CALDON LOW

"And where have you been, my Mary,
    And where have you been from me?"
"I have been to the top of the Caldon Low,
    The midsummer night to see."

"And what did you see, my Mary,
    All up on the Caldon Low?"
"I saw the glad sunshine come down,
    And I saw the merry winds blow."

"And what did you hear, my Mary,
    All up on the Caldon Hill?"
"I heard the drops of water made,
    And the ears of the green corn fill."

"Oh, tell me all, my Mary—
    All, all that ever you know;
For you must have seen the fairies,
    Last night, on the Caldon Low."

"Then take me on your knee, mother;
    And listen, mother of mine;
A hundred fairies danced last night,
    And the harpers they were nine;

"And their harp strings rung so merrily
      To their dancing feet so small;
But oh, the words of their talking
      Were merrier far than all."

"And what were the words, my Mary,
      That then you heard them say?"
"I 'll tell you all, my mother;
      But let me have my way.

"Some of them played with the water,
      And rolled it down the hill;
'And this,' they said, 'shall speedily turn
      The poor old miller's mill;

" 'For there has been no water
      Ever since the first of May;
And a busy man will the miller be
      At dawning of the day.

" 'Oh, the miller, how he will laugh
      When he sees the mill dam rise!
The jolly old miller, how he will laugh
      Till the tears fill both his eyes.'

"And some they seized the little winds
      That sounded over the hill;
And each put a horn into his mouth,
      And blew both loud and shrill;

" 'And there,' they said, 'the merry winds go
    Away from every horn;
And they shall clear the mildew dank
    From the blind old widow's corn.

" 'Oh, the poor, blind widow,
    Though she has been blind so long,
She 'll be blithe enough when the mildew 's gone,
    And the corn stands tall and strong.'

"And some they brought the brown lint seed,
    And flung it down from the Low;
'And this,' they said, 'by the sunrise,
    In the weaver's croft shall grow.

" 'Oh, the poor, lame weaver,
    How he will laugh outright,
When he sees his dwindling flax field
    All full of flowers by night!'

"And then outspoke a brownie,
    With a long beard on his chin:
'I have spun up all the tow,' said he,
    'And I want some more to spin.

" 'I 've spun a piece of hempen cloth,
    And I want to spin another;
A little sheet for Mary's bed,
    And an apron for her mother.'

"With that I could not help but laugh,
    And I laughed out loud and free;
And then on the top of the Caldon Low
    There was no one left but me.

"And all on the top of the Caldon Low
    The mists were cold and gray,
And nothing I saw but the mossy stones,
    That round about me lay.

"But, coming down from the hilltop,
    I heard afar below,
How busy the jolly miller was,
    And how the wheel did go.

"And I peeped into the widow's field,
    And, sure enough, were seen
The yellow ears of the mildewed corn
    All standing stout and green.

"And down by the weaver's croft I stole,
    To see if the flax were sprung;
And I met the weaver at his gate,
    With the good news on his tongue!

"Now this is all I heard, mother,
    And all that I did see;
So, pr'ythee, make my bed, mother,
    For I 'm tired as I can be."

—MARY HOWITT.

111

THE UNSEEN PLAYMATE

When children are playing alone on the green,
    In comes the playmate that never was seen.
When children are happy and lonely and good,
    The Friend of the Children comes out of the wood.

Nobody heard him and nobody saw,
    His is a picture you never could draw,
But he 's sure to be present, abroad or at home,
    When children are happy and playing alone.

He lies in the laurels, he runs on the grass,
    He sings when you tinkle the musical glass;
Whene'er you are happy and cannot tell why,
    The Friend of the Children is sure to be by!

He loves to be little, he hates to be big,
    'T is he that inhabits the caves that you dig;
'T is he when you play with your soldiers of tin
    That sides with the Frenchmen and never can win.

'T is he, when at night you go off to your bed,
    Bids you go to sleep and not trouble your head;
For whenever they 're lying, in cupboard or shelf,
    'T is he will take care of your playthings himself!
                —ROBERT LOUIS STEVENSON.

HIAWATHA'S CHILDHOOD

THE HOME OF HIAWATHA

By the shores of Gitche Gumee,
By the shining Big-Sea-Water,
Stood the wigwam of Nokomis,
Daughter of the Moon, Nokomis.
Dark behind it rose the forest,
Rose the black and gloomy pine trees,
Rose the firs with cones upon them;
Bright before it beat the water,
Beat the clear and sunny water,
Beat the shining Big-Sea-Water.
    There the wrinkled old Nokomis
Nursed the little Hiawatha,
Rocked him in his linden cradle,
Bedded soft in moss and rushes,
Safely bound with reindeer sinews;
Stilled his fretful wail by saying,
"Hush! the Naked Bear will hear thee!"
Lulled him into slumber, singing,
"Ewa-yea! my little owlet!
Who is this, that lights the wigwam?
With his great eyes lights the wigwam?
Ewa-yea! my little owlet!"

THE STARS

Many things Nokomis taught him
Of the stars that shine in heaven;
Showed him Ishkoodah, the comet,
Ishkoodah, with fiery tresses;
Showed the Death Dance of the spirits,
Warriors with their plumes and war clubs,
Flaring far away to northward
In the frosty nights of Winter:
Showed the broad white road in heaven,
Pathway of the ghosts, the shadows,
Running straight across the heavens,
Crowded with the ghosts, the shadows.

THE FIREFLY

At the door on summer evenings
Sat the little Hiawatha;
Heard the whispering of the pine trees,
Heard the lapping of the waters,
Sounds of music, words of wonder;
"Minne-wawa!" said the pine trees,
"Mudway-aushka!" said the water.
Saw the firefly, Wah-wah-taysee,
Flitting through the dusk of evening,
With the twinkle of its candle
Lighting up the brakes and bushes,
And he sang the song of children,
Sang the song Nokomis taught him:

"Wah-wah-taysee, little firefly,
Little, flitting, white-fire insect,
Little, dancing, white-fire creature,
Light me with your little candle,
Ere upon my bed I lay me,
Ere in sleep I close my eyelids!"

THE LADY IN THE MOON

Saw the moon rise from the water
Rippling, rounding from the water,
Saw the flecks and shadows on it,
Whispered, "What is that, Nokomis?"
And the good Nokomis answered:
"Once a warrior, very angry,
Seized his grandmother, and threw her
Up into the sky at midnight;
Right against the moon he threw her;
'T is her body that you see there."

THE RAINBOW

Saw the rainbow in the heaven,
In the eastern sky, the rainbow
Whispered, "What is that, Nokomis?"
And the good Nokomis answered:
" 'T is the heaven of flowers you see there;
All the wild flowers of the forest,
All the lilies of the prairie,
When on earth they fade and perish,
Blossom in that heaven above us."

HIAWATHA'S CHICKENS

When he heard the owls at midnight,
Hooting, laughing in the forest,
"What is that?" he cried in terror,
"What is that," he said, "Nokomis?"
And the good Nokomis answered:
"That is but the owl and owlet,
Talking in their native language,
Talking, scolding at each other."
Then the little Hiawatha
Learned of every bird its language,
Learned their names and all their secrets,
How they built their nests in Summer,
Where they hid themselves in Winter,
Talked with them whene'er he met them,
Called them "Hiawatha's Chickens."

HIAWATHA'S BROTHERS

Of all beasts he learned the language,
Learned their names and all their secrets,
How the beavers built their lodges,
Where the squirrels hid their acorns,
How the reindeer ran so swiftly,
Why the rabbit was so timid,
Talked with them whene'er he met them,
Called them "Hiawatha's Brothers."
—HENRY WADSWORTH LONGFELLOW.

116

THE PLAINT OF THE CAMEL

Canary birds feed on sugar and seed,
　　Parrots have crackers to crunch;
And as for the poodles, they tell me the noodles
　　Have chickens and cream for their lunch.
　　　　But there 's never a question
　　　　About *my* digestion—
　　Anything does for me!

Cats, you 're aware, can repose in a chair,
　　Chickens can roost upon rails;
Puppies are able to sleep in a stable,
　　And oysters can slumber in pails.
　　　　But no one supposes
　　　　A poor Camel dozes—
　　Any place does for me!

Lambs are inclosed where it 's never exposed,
　　Coops are constructed for hens;
Kittens are treated to houses well heated,
　　And pigs are protected by pens.
　　　　But a Camel comes handy
　　　　Wherever it 's sandy—
　　Anywhere does for me!

People would laugh if you rode a giraffe
    Or mounted the back of an ox;
It 's nobody's habit to ride on a rabbit
    Or try to bestraddle a fox.
        But as for a Camel, he 's
        Ridden by families—
    Any load does for me!

A snake is as round as a hole in the ground,
    And weasels are wavy and sleek;
And no alligator could ever be straighter
    Than lizards that live in a creek,
        But a Camel 's all lumpy
        And bumpy and humpy—
    Any shape does for me!
                    —CHARLES EDWARD CARRYL.

NONSENSE VERSE

There was an old man who said, "How
Shall I flee from this horrible cow?
    I will sit on this stile
    And continue to smile,
Which may soften the heart of the cow."
                    —EDWARD LEAR.

LITTLE BILLEE

There were three sailors of Bristol city
    Who took a boat and went to sea.
But first with beef and captain's biscuits
    And pickled pork they loaded she.

There was gorging Jack and guzzling Jimmy,
    And the youngest he was little Billee,
Now when they got as far as the Equator,
    They 'd nothing left but one split pea.

Says gorging Jack to guzzling Jimmy,
    "I am extremely hungaree."
To gorging Jack says guzzling Jimmy,
    "We 've nothing left, us must eat we."

Says gorging Jack to guzzling Jimmy,
    "With one another, we should n't agree!
There 's little Bill he 's young and tender,
    We 're old and tough, so let 's eat he.

"Oh! Billy, we 're going to kill and eat you,
    So undo the button of your chemie."
When Bill received this information
    He used his pocket-handerchie.

"First let me say my catechism,
    Which my poor mammy taught to me."
"Make haste, make haste," says guzzling Jimmy,
    While Jack pulled out his snickersnee.

So Billy went up to the main-top gallant mast,
    And down he fell on his bended knee.
He scarce had come to the twelfth commandment
    When up he jumps. "There 's land I see.

"Jerusalem and Madagascar,
    And North and South Amerikee:
There 's the British flag a riding at anchor,
    With Admiral Napier, K.C.B."

So when they got aboard of the Admiral's
    He hanged fat Jack and flogged Jimmy:
But as for little Bill he made him
    The Captain of a Seventy-three.
                            —WILLIAM MAKEPEACE THACKERAY.

120

A NAUTICAL BALLAD

A capital ship for an ocean trip,
  Was the Walloping Window-Blind.
No gale that blew dismayed her crew,
  Nor troubled the captain's mind.

The man at the wheel was taught to feel
  Contempt for the wildest blow;
And it often appeared—when the weather had cleared—
  He had been in his bunk below.

The boatswain's mate was very sedate,
  Yet fond of amusement too;
And he played hopscotch with the starboard watch,
  While the captain tickled the crew.

And the gunner we had was apparently mad,
  For he sat on the after-rail
And fired salutes with the captain's boots
  In the teeth of the booming gale.

The captain sat on the commodore's hat,
  And dined in a royal way,
Off toasted pigs and pickles and figs
  And gunnery bread each day.

The cook was Dutch and behaved as such,
  For the diet he gave the crew,
Was a number of tons of hot cross-buns,
  Served up with sugar and glue.

All nautical pride we laid aside,
  And we cast our vessel ashore,
On the Gulliby Isles, where the Poo-Poo smiles
  And the Rumpletum-Bunders roar.

We sat on the edge of a sandy ledge,
  And shot at the whistling bee:
And the cinnamon bats wore waterproof hats,
  As they danced by the sounding sea.

On Rug-gub bark, from dawn till dark,
  We fed, till we all had grown
Uncommonly shrunk; when a Chinese junk
  Came in from the Torriby Zone.

She was stubby and square, but we didn't much care,
  So we cheerily put to sea;
And we left the crew of the junk to chew,
  The bark of the Rug-gub tree.

THE SEA

The Sea is a good friend of mine;
    For when I come along,
She makes her ripples dance for glee
    And sings a splendid song.
Down close beside her I can watch
    The silver sails unfurl,
And every rolling, tumbling wave
    Upon the shore uncurl;—
They make wide mirrors for the sky
    And zig-zag ropes of sand,
To mark the farthest edges where
    The water touches land.

At night the Moon a pathway makes
    Across the spreading Sea;
It must be for the Sea's mermaids
    And small mermen, and me.
It leads straight from its skyward end
    To ripples at my feet,
And sometime I perchance may trip
    Along the golden street;
I'd like to visit with the Moon
    And walk the Milky Way
And linger with the little stars—
    If the golden path would stay!

THE MERMAN

Who would be
A merman bold,
Sitting alone,
Singing alone
Under the sea,
With a crown of gold,
On a throne?
 I would be a merman bold;
I would sit and sing the whole of the day;
I would fill the sea-halls with a voice of power;
But at night I would roam abroad and play
With the mermaids in and out of the rocks,
Dressing their hair with the white sea-flower;
And then we would wander away, away
To the pale-green sea-groves straight and high,
  Chasing each other merrily.

Who would be
A mermaid fair,
Singing alone,
Combing her hair
Under the sea,
In a golden curl,
With a comb of pearl,
On a throne?

I would be a mermaid fair,
I would sing to myself the whole of the day;
With a comb of pearl I would comb my hair.
I would comb my hair till my ringlets would fall
    Low adown, low adown,
From under my starry sea-bud crown
And I should look like a fountain of gold
    Springing alone,
    With a shrill inner sound,
    Over the throne.

        —ALFRED TENNYSON.

THE LORD IS MY SHEPHERD

The Lord is my shepherd; I shall not want.
He maketh me to lie down in green pastures;
He leadeth me beside the still waters;
He restoreth my soul.
He leadeth me in the paths of righteousness for His
    name's sake.
Yea, though I walk through the valley of the shadow of
    death,
I will fear no evil, for Thou art with me.
Thy rod and Thy staff they comfort me.
Thou preparest a table before me in the presence of mine
    enemies;
Thou anointest my head with oil, my cup runneth over.
Surely goodness and mercy shall follow me all the days of
    my life.
And I will dwell in the house of the Lord forever.

—*Psalm* xxiii.

AMERICA

My country, 't is of thee,
Sweet land of liberty,
    Of thee I sing;
Land where my fathers died,
Land of the pilgrims' pride,
From every mountain-side
    Let freedom ring.

My native country, thee,
Land of the noble free,
    Thy name I love;
I love thy rocks and rills,
Thy woods and templed hills,
My heart with rapture thrills
    Like that above.

Let music swell the breeze,
And ring from all the trees,
    Sweet freedom's song;
Let mortal tongues awake,
Let all that breathe partake,
Let rocks their silence break—
    The sound prolong.

Our fathers' God, to Thee,
Author of liberty,
    To Thee we sing,

Long may our land be bright
With freedom's holy light;
Protect us by thy might,
Great God, our King.
—S<small>AMUEL</small> F<small>RANCIS</small> S<small>MITH</small>.

COLUMBIA, THE GEM OF THE OCEAN

O Columbia, the gem of the ocean,
The home of the brave and the free,
The shrine of each patriot's devotion,
A world offers homage to thee.
Thy mandates make heroes assemble,
When Liberty's form stands in view;
Thy banners make tyranny tremble—
When borne by the red, white, and blue!

When borne by the red, white, and blue,
When borne by the red, white, and blue,
Thy banners make tyranny tremble,
When borne by the red, white, and blue.

When war winged its wide desolation,
And threatened the land to deform,
The ark then of Freedom's foundation,
Columbia, rode safe through the storm;
With her garlands of vict'ry around her,
When so bravely she bore her brave crew,
With her flag proudly floating before her,
The boast of the red, white, and blue.

THE WATCHMAN'S SONG

Listen, children, hear me tell,
Ten now tolls from the old church bell.
Once were given commandments ten,
To be always kept by men.

Naught avails that men should ward us,—
One will watch and One will guard us,
May He, of His boundless night,
Give unto us all "good night."

Listen, children, hear me tell,
Eleven now tolls from the old church bell.
Eleven Apostles went there forth,
Preaching truth through all the earth.

Listen, children, hear me tell,
Twelve now tolls from the old church bell.
Twelve hours day, and twelve hours night,
Time to order all things right.

Listen, children, hear me tell,
One now tolls from the old church bell.
One hath made the world, and He
Orders all things righteously.

Listen, children, hear me tell,
Two now strikes on the old church bell.
Two ways lie in each man's sight,—
May you, children, choose the right.

Listen, children, hear me tell,
Three now strikes on the old church bell.
Three times think when you 're in doubt,
Ere you set your task about.

Listen, children, hear me tell,
Four now strikes on the old church bell.
Four sides hath the plowed field,—
May thy life, child, harvest yield.

Now the stars must fade away,
Quickly now will come the day:
Children, thank the bounteous Power
That doth guard you every hour.

Naught avails that man should ward you,
One doth watch and One doth guard you;
He hath, of His bounteous might,
Given unto you all "good night."

INDEX TO FIRST LINES

131

132

INDEX OF AUTHORS

135

136

CPSIA information can be obtained at www.ICGtesting.com
234094LV00001B/376/A